I0481215

Contents

About the Author

Highly accomplished IT professional offering 10 years of experience in all aspects of technical project management, business applications, and information systems.

Geographical information systems, Intelligent transport systems and managerial information systems, Track record in managing and creating new technology projects using multiple technologies. Participating in the design and implementation of complete life cycles.

Worked as an employee, senior employee, a leader and an entrepreneur.

Lived between Cairo, Egypt, and Jeddah, Saudi Arabia. Both cities influenced my inspiration in many different ways, ones with the great history and epical atmosphere in the great city of Cairo, and another time with the charming city of Jeddah where everything is actually inspired by the wonderful red sea.

Husband for a lovely wife and father for a gorgeous 8 years daughter. I love reading books, listening to almost all types of music. Plying football and table tennis. Traveled to many countries and I wish if I can travel more, I believe that each country, each city have something to see or something to smell or maybe something to taste that might change something in your life for the better.

Author's note

Thank you for reading this book, it is a pleasure and owner that you are interested to read my writings.

I wrote this book based on my personal experience dealing with people as a family member, employee and a leader. I have been through the experience of reading and analyzing everyone and everything around, I wrote a lot of notes and read a lot of books in addition to self-development courses for more than ten years. I have decided to expose in writing all that I have learned throughout these years with others and I will be really happy if what I write really helps.

Before writing this first book, I used to write all the time and keep what I write for myself.

I used to write notes, mini-novels, and many other things.

I would like to take this opportunity to thank my wife "The love of my life", family and all of my friends.

I would like to thank my work colleagues and partners for the great and valuables inputs they incorporated into my soul. A full book would not be enough to say thanks to everyone I suppose to say thanks to.

I would really appreciate if you share your thoughts and feedback about what I wrote in this book and in any other book.

This book is a dedication to my mother's soul.

Ahmed M. Sonbol

ahmedm.sonbol@gmail.com

Introduction

The world has changed since great inventions. The day to day life is full of routine activities that we do without thinking. It is very common that we only follow and do things that work. Our modern life has changed us into consumers of everything. We are unconsciously attached to what we do, and we cannot live without it anymore. This has distracted us, and grabbed us from being initiative takers, thinking out of the box, innovative and creative. Creativity is not only artwork and not only TV ads or media content. Creativity can be and should be what drives everyone's life.

If you are reading this book now maybe you are lucky. It is important that you stop whatever goes around to drive you and stay without looking at the chances and potentials you may have if you added creativity into account. Many great inventions or achievements in the human history were because of creative thinking, from people who decided to cut out routine or copying others and thought of an alternative way. I wish this book will help readers awaken the creative thinkers inside them before their creativity dies following life flows.

This book is intended to force reader's attention to their negative attitudes or mindsets in which they stay attached and not able to think creatively. The other important intention of this book is to guide you to some simple creative thinking techniques that will inspire you to start a new life.

Let's Start

The first thing you need to think about before we go into a lot of how to think creatively, you need to be aware of two keywords attitude & mindset. Your attitude toward your life and what goes wrong in your personal or professional lives is your start point. Psychologists say that only 10% of what happens to you in your life is out of your own control, 90% is based on how you reacted or dealt with it.

Well if you are blaming anything or anyone around you for a drawback or a failure in your life, please don't do that. Great people did their phenomenal achievements in the most disappointing moments of their life. It is the art of transforming negative vibes into positive power.

These are not only words, if your flight is delayed and you have to stay a couple of more hours in the airport for nothing, it is you who will decide either you will go shouting with airlines staff and sit somewhere angry drinking coffee or smoking. Or you will think of the best use of your time and learn something new or think of solutions for any of your problems.

Most of the time, negative things happen to us give us a great chance that we usually don't utilize. When you feel that there is nothing to lose anymore, your mind opens the doors to new perspectives. You will think in the way that you were usually afraid of, as long as you aren't in your comfort zone. All depends on your personal decision.

Mindset, it is how you used to think how things happen, work or created. What is possible and what is not possible. Great ideas were killed because of assumptions or methods people used to perform and follow. If Galileo had followed what was assumed in his time, he would never discover planets and scientific revolutions that we are still using and relying on until the moment. Be open to explore and doubt. Listening to different voices and even the most contradicting ones with your own thoughts expands your vision.

Perfection is in imperfection

Seeking perfection might be an enormous mistake in a man's life. If you wait for everything to be in the right place, everything to be exactly as you wanted to be, everything as planned, you end up with nothing or out of time. We get exhausted seeking perfection and forget to look around us and see the beauty of perfection in imperfection everywhere around. Babies are angles from heaven, but they cry and get sick from time to time. Flowers maybe one of the most beautiful creatures you can see but they may have thorns. Nature is the mother of beauty and perfection, perfection in its deeper meaning. Imperfection brings the natural touch and feel of everything in our life. This is not about standards or any other technical aspects of doing things the right way, it is about how we see our outcomes and evaluate where we stand from our goals and dreams in life. The perfection has a different definition from one person to another, you don't know if your perfect is what your boss, audience or customers want. Many great painters regretted their paintings because they thought it is not good enough, most of these paintings are considered the most extraordinary artwork in the history of all times. Perfectionists are most potentially disappointed for not meeting their expectations, take advantage of imperfections and adapt yourself to accept unplanned or unwanted outcomes. Hard work and products made with passion and love are good candidates for success. Always remember that humans are not perfect, force imperfections to melt and complement into your product, your artwork, your painting or into your day to day job.

Ignite your inspiration

Look around and explore what inspires you. Everyone has his own keys of self-motivation and inspiration. These are not secrets, our rapid rhythm daily life has affected our ability to sense and enjoy what we do for a living. Some people have no time to enjoy the food they eat, eye-catching sceneries around them, and not even the simplest emotions they can exchange with people close to them. It is never too late, there is always something that you enjoy doing or experiencing in life. As a start, don't let things pass without you feel them. Pay attention to your food and enjoy the taste, take a deep breath and smell nice things around essences, delicious food or the smell of nature surrounding you. It makes big difference in your life, this will positively slow down your life base and make you see and do things out of a completely different emotional state. People with less tension are happier and more productive. Starting from there you will be able to identify your passion about what you do for a living, it might be the same thing that you do every day and this will help you reach out to your optimum performance and exceed even your own personal expectations. And it might be something else, this will help you identify it. Everyone has a talent inside him, don't leave your talent berried in your soul. Doing the thing that you love to do is defiantly where you can explore the best of your capabilities. Again it is not only about being a writer or a painter, it is not only artwork. Business could be your passion, you could be a talented surgeon or a scientist that will change the world with an astonishing invention. It is possible that you need a break to explore yourself, please do it. Set goals for yourself without specifying outcomes! Yes, sometimes specifying goals limits your vision. The sky is your limit.

Be a Leader

Don't be surprised, yes you have to be. Even if it is not your position in life you need to take leadership as an attitude when it comes to creative thinking. Every one of us is a leader of something. You can be a leader at work, leader at home or at least leader of yourself. When leadership is your attitude, you will tempt to lead yourself or your team to achieve your goals.

The first step of the way is a sharp desire to go really far. This is what you need leadership for, a leader will take himself and everyone involved the way long until they achieve what they wanted in the first place. You don't have to know everything, leadership is about leading others or yourself to explore new ways of doing things. Inventions came out of people who thought of alternatives and explore new perspectives of getting things done or why things around them actually happen. Leadership as an attitude will drive you on the way to the point. Creative thinkers are leaders in their heart and soul. Leaders are accountable for their failures, there is no great success in life without failing before it. Failures drive leaders to challenge obstacles in their way. Failures are leader's motivation engine which illuminates their darkness and takes them beyond expectations.

Explore and doubt

Creativity requires not to stop at any one's conclusion. Read more, ask for people contribution. Asking people around to contribute is a great setup for a creative environment. When people feel that they are welcomed to express their ideas, they will add an amazing value to your project. Creative ideas might be in anyone's head, be the explorer. Go the extra mile and explore unusual methods of doing what you are aiming to do. Don't be tied to the right way of doing it, it is true that there is always a right way of doing things. This is exactly what everybody around is actually doing. It takes a creative explorer to find out the extraordinary. Always feed your exploration desire with reading about what you love to do, meeting new people worked or thought about your ideas. A creative person has to doubt "positively" if you don't doubt what everyone is regularly doing you will stop before exploring new things. You need to doubt not only what people said it works, what didn't work with other people could be your start point. Creativity is to be open to all possibilities. Don't stop to explore and doubt. If you love what you do, you will enjoy the journey. All opinions worth to be considered, explore all thoughts even from the most contradicting streams. Seeing the big picture will allow you to emerge. The greatest scientists of all time history didn't sleep at night or did whatever it takes to come up with theories or great inventions. Great people didn't leave anything in their life to just pass without wondering, they lived their life exploring and doubting everything goes around. The most interesting and influential thinker of the fifth century Socrates used to doubt. Socrates was known for asking people questions and making them reach a conclusion on their own. The great philosopher did nothing but doubting and exploring people minds, his questioning habit made his great history of philosophy and wisdom.

Find a competitor

Having a competitor is very healthy for your creative journey. Competing in the right way will take your thoughts and ideas to another level. As good and powerful your competitors are, as much as you step forward to reach your outstanding achievements. Competition is a great nutrition for success. Bill Gates once decided to help Apple with financial aid when they were suffering from financial issues. Steve Jobs was the best competitor for Bill Gates in the information technology business. Bill Gates didn't want to lose his best competitor which might impact his desire to perform and do more for his business. Yes, to this extent. Be aware of whom are you competing with, no one likes a boring one-sided football game. Victory is even greater when you have powerful competitors coming after you. Do you know that the owners of Adidas and Puma are brothers? Yes, Adolf and Rudolf are German brothers who decided back between 1945 and 1949 to start exactly the same type of business.

Adidas became surly competing with Puma and this what made them the valuable brands we know today. Take advantage of your strong competitors and give even more.

Never too early or too late

Creativity is not limited to any age. Little kids may be a great source of astonishing ideas. Creativity has strong links to nature. Young kids are to the manner born. They are capable of initiating creative thinking without they know it. As an experienced adult, don't ever think that it is too late to start. Life changing ideas could come at any point in your life. It depends on you if you decided to think differently. Don't lose your motivation because of time, you don't know what the best time to start for yourself is. There are quite enough stories about people who succeeded after a long journey of doing something else. The creator of X-Men, Spider-Man the great Stan Lee wrote his first on the 39th birthday. After being a journalist for most of her career Vera Wang entered the fashion world at the age of 40, today she is one of the world's most important designers. Henry Ford created his revolutionary T Model car at his 45th birthday. There is no excuse, age or disability never been an obstacle for most of the great inventors, scientists or artists throughout history.

Mother Nature

Nature is the origin of creativity and inspiration. Have you ever looked around and speculated how everything in this world is perfectly working together with everything else without being perfect in itself. God has created most of the perfection of the imperfections. It is where we are living. If you look and think of how animals are living their lives, how plants are growing and reproduce, how birds are living and protecting their little ones. Before the discovery of engineering, medicine, physics or chemistry by humans. God had perfectly planted these sciences into his creatures. The way birds or animals securing their food, protecting and rearing their young, or the way they mate and breed. It is all spectacularly engineered together. Nature is a perfect source of creativity. Back to nature, back to roots. This is where you find purity and virginity. Nature has been inspiring a lot of creative thinkers. Most of the exceptional architects like Gaudi were inspired and influenced by nature. Start where creativity is in every detail of details.

Awaken your subconscious (The treasure within you)

Your subconscious is a spectacular virtual world. Are you aware that you have another world deep inside of you?

Everyone has this parallel world living subconsciously. A world with different possibilities, a world with no limitations. It might have its own creatures, its own nature, or it might have its own creativity. Unfortunately, as we grow we were taught and influenced not to listen to this world. Dreams come only from there. Dreams! Wait a minute, do you dream? Do you know that most of the adults I know rarely dream while sleeping? We have lost our entry visa to our own imaginary world. This is a world we lived in and loved in our childhood. All children are often dreaming and expressing about their subconscious ideas and characters. They feed it with their virgin appetite to explore and imagine. They live in it until we educate them not to do so. A lot of creativity is deep in your soul. Being told what to do eventually hides your virtual world. Thinking itself could be the worst trap for creativity, we were influenced to think and do things by book "As it should be". We stopped our imagination, we berried our parallel world. Set yourself free of life's constraints, release your mind to your soul, ask the little kid inside you to think instead of you do it. Learn how to relax and open your vision to a different perspective on everything, listen to the sound inside of you that you used to ignore.

We ignore our inner voices because we are afraid of others reactions or how society will see us after we expose our ideas. Listen to your inner voice, awaken your subconscious, be part of your own virtual world. Don't waste your time looking for the treasure, the treasure is within you.

Doers Dreamers

Dreaming is great. A man with no dream is lost. Dreams are blessings from heaven, dreams are the sound of our inner voice and subconscious world. The problem is that we stop at dreaming, how many people you met told you about his dream job or business. Everyone has a school time dream which eventually turns into another mature dream after college. How many of these did actually take a step forward and chase his dreams? There is a thin line between having great life dreams and our ability to convert them into achievements or even failures. It is ok to fail, it is a weakness not to try. Dream big and do bigger, a man with a dream must be a man with a plan. It is the thing that you've been thinking all of your time and not doing, is what you should do.

Crossing boundaries might not be an easy task for most of us, most of the time we are locked in comfort zones. Keep in mind that your decision to start is a great start. If you want to change your life for the better, it doesn't mean that you need to change everything.

It is a state of mind you created for yourself. The keys to successful personal or professional lives are most probably are in our pockets. Don't blame your situation, circumstances, and people around you or where you are.

Doers just do it, the decision starts inside you. Face yourself, the way how people around sees you, might not be what you feel for yourself and that is exactly where you should start. Stop yourself from blaming, whenever you are blaming anyone or anything, stop yourself immediately and remember that this is a lifetime mistake. Set with yourself and think of solutions, think of what you did wrong and don't do it again. Much more than 50% of a problem resolution is the courage to face it. The most negative image of you in anyone's mind should be your top motivator to breakthrough. Break the ice between yourself and your dreams, take the initiative to explore them and turn them into actions.

These are only words

Ok. If this idea came to your mind when you read the previous part of this book. If you thought that nothing is going to change following any of what previously said. If you are not yet convinced with any of them told stories about successful people in history. Well, it is not easy to switch from a negative state of mind to a positive one. Negativity is a poison, sneaks into our souls, spreads like a cancer cell and dominates like a king on his throne.

Detox your soul from negative vibes, every time you think in a negative way, remember it is a negative poison. Take a deep breath and force yourself to use your energy in a positive thought. Don't fall into a negative trap, stay away from anyone trying to direct you to the other way around. You will never regret changing your mind to positive, stop overthinking, and see the positive side of everything. Take the advantage of the half-full water glass and drink it. You don't have to think of the empty half, it will not help your thirst. Did you visualize that? The sun is burning, the weather is hot. A glass half filled with water standing right there, one person found it and said, it is half empty and not enough. Another person came after and directly drunk it and said, thank god it has water. One will leave angry and thirsty, and the other one will feel satisfied and happy.

Happiness starts with how do you see and evaluate what happens to you in your life. If they informed you in the morning that you are fired, you have two options. The first is to be sad and depressed and don't know what to do. And the other option is to think that it might be the time to leave the job. It might be the sign that you need to change and look for something better for yourself. Different results are guaranteed. The first gentleman will take time to recover, will wait for someone to help and might be in trouble. The 2nd gentleman will go find a new job, will work on himself to develop. Will start a new life at some point.

Always remember that the decision was yours. If there is no ups and downs in your life, it means you are dead. Take the ups upper, and take the downs up and don't let yourself down. The great Beethoven faced the worst disappointment in a musician's career when he faced the hearing problem.

Just because he decided to win the battle and overcome his hearing issue, he came up with his masterpiece the 9th symphony after he completely lost his hearing. Impossible is nothing, stories can fill in your life reading. The decision is yours.

Idea Factory

It is the time now to start with tactics. First, set up your idea factory, charge your batteries, lighten up the darkness and start up the engines. If you need to come up with one idea, work on finding much more. This strategy will help not being attached to one approach of thinking.

Forcing your mind to explore a lot more. By the time you will learn how to think differently each and every time. Creativity takes more than one idea, it takes going beyond ordinary thinking. Great painters used to paint much more paintings for the same feeling, each one has its own unique beauty. For them they though people will not like what they paint every time they decide to paint another one. This is what creative thinkers are about.

Creativity has no limits, extraordinary visions and unlimited techniques or methods. Get everyone engaged and feed the creativity machines, don't stop your production lines so quickly. Ideas might inspire better ideas, the first idea is only the start. It is against creativity to fall into the first idea trap, you will get attached to it and will not be able to come up with something better. Don't forget to explore and doubt. The factory operation has a direct relation to the nature of your thinking environment. Creativity comes when no one is afraid or shy to express his ideas, all equivalently. No discrimination based on roles or education. As healthy as your working environment is, you will be able to produce beyond anyone's expectations. Encourage criticism, maybe you don't need to follow all negative opinions about your ideas or work, but it is very important to evaluate all positive and negative thoughts and analyze them, incorporate big or small modifications for better.

Don't Compromise

Stay determined to your goal, sharp when it comes to your choices. Don't leave room to comprise reaching your objectives, or the quality you planned for your work, the hard work success would deserve or creative thinking. Compromise is only a start for losing track, walking backward to square zero. When you don't compromise you either work more or work better, you will always look forward to more.

Knowing precisely what you are aiming to achieve solids your actions, adds value to its purpose and gives a deeper meaning.

Make sure that your objectives are clear in every step of your journey. Always remember what quality you desired for what you do or need. Success is a package, it comes when all components are perfectly designed, combined and harmonized together.

Rework is what creative people do. Great writers used to rework what they wrote, every time it comes with better wording or phrases. If you look at what you did and your mind didn't come up with a new idea this mean you stopped being creative. Creative minds always have something to add, it is a stream of thoughts comes out of the passion and love they have for what they do.

Rework doesn't mean that you should stay in an endless loop of redoing your work, creative thinkers will know when to stop. Every time you think what you did before will inspire you to be more creative. You only need to start, you cannot edit an empty page. Creative thinkers tempt to rethink what other people thought of, it ignites their passion for producing new or better ideas. Rework has never been a disappointment, if you think of changes or implementing your work in a different technique, don't miss the chance of being more creative.

Curiosity

Education, innovation, and artwork are all in the best shape if you are curious. Curiosity is an anti-monotone treatment. If you are curious to learn, explore and understand. You will be the best candidate to innovate and produce phenomenal creative thinking.

Curiosity was the main reason behind all of the great explorations and inventions in the mankind history. Creative thinkers are curious to know when, why and how things happen. Curiosity drives creative thinkers to dig deep into facts and details and extract a lot more of everything. Curiosity takes creative thinkers to the next level, if you are curious, there will be the next level at all times.

What ordinary people call innovation is curiosity added to the passion and desire to break through ordinary. Curiosity is not something that you can go to school for, and it is not knowledge. Curiosity is the man's tool to learn, explore, achieve and innovate. Make curiosity to be your best habit, your sword to fight against your own fears. Curiosity makes you different in your daily life if you started to feel curious about what goes around you in your school, college or work. You will start finding your way to step ahead of others. You will start to explore more about what you do, you will get closer to standout and shine with your passion to learn and share more with people around you. Nothing easier than being curious, you just need to feel it.

Tell ego to go sleep

The most common reason why we don't attempt to experience new things is our ego. Ego is the barrier when it comes to creativity. Creative thinkers have to be open, flexible and modest.

Creative people have absolutely no problem to learn or explore, with or from anyone. They enjoy finding out alternative thinking and methods because of their openness and freedom toward all options, opinions, and possibilities.

Knowing the value of yourself is important. A great vision, mission, and achievements are all good to have. Nevertheless, transforming all of what previously mentioned to be your own big prison, is not what you need for your life. The more down to earth, you are, the more you get closer to people, alternative ways, and endless solutions. Freedom is where every great thing starts from, don't put yourself in your own jail.

Creativity starts with a deep feeling of freedom, a freedom to think, to walk the extra mile and go beyond expectations.

Freedom is what drives a creative thinker to the world of unknowns, a world of new probabilities and possibilities. The world where innovation is created and extraordinary achievements come to life. When you feel that you are free of your fears to fail or your fears about how the society will react to what you do, it is your perfect time to perform. Don't let your ego prevent you from reaching out great potentials that you may experience in your life. If you decided to think creatively and to experience the best that you can do for your life, lock up your ego in a jail before it does it for you.

Time to balance

If you are doing what you really love, if what you do is what inspires you to reach out your top performance and self-confidence, you will not need to break. Most of the people thinking for a long time about taking a break from what they do because they are not feeling comfortable anymore are not doing what they really love to do. If you are doing what you really love, what you really own a great passion for, you will never feel tired or bored doing it. You will always feel excited to give more for what you love to do, you will enjoy every single step of your way.

A creative thinker will not need to balance work and life, his enjoyment of what he is doing is what makes him satisfied. A great passion for what you do for life enlighten your soul to feel better about your life and forces this positive feeling to spread to everyone around. Balancing in terms of time management might be a different thing, however, as much as you give for what you love to do, as much as you will be able to give to your personal life, as long as you found yourself in it.

It will never be the necessity or the desire of disconnecting yourself away from your work life. It will never be because of your stressfulness or tensions that you are suffering from. Nothing better relieving life pressure than being yourself, succeeding in what you love to do for life.

Nothing comparable to victory for great knights, nothing more memorable than scoring a goal in the last minute and turning the game upside down for football player, nothing more satisfying than performing a successful sophisticated hurt surgery for a surgeon. Visualize and imagine a previous couple of lines, since the fascinating feeling of getting what you love doing. This glamorous feeling is unforgivable, always remember these lines if you felt down or inadequate. This remarkable taste of honor is what keeps you starving for more success, always feeling positive about yourself, feeling happier and more satisfied in your personal life. You will never consume your mind in any negative way anymore, every one of us is special and precious in their hurt and soul in some way or another. It is how we live our life what changes the outcomes from hell to heaven both on earth.

Balance, time management or being organized all are great things but they have nothing to do with what I said here. You will always need to learn how to manage your own business. Nevertheless, it is what you feel about what you do is what makes the difference your life experience. Make sure that you are doing what you meant to do you, be stubborn to success, and remember the magical recipe of senses. Balance is what you get for granted.

It is all about presentation

You eat with your eyes first. It is how man and women behave, we like beauty. A dish cooked by the best chef in the world might not be touched if it is not presented in the proper way. A nicely shaped and organized dish will trigger your appetite to eat without thinking. This difference is what we call presentation.

The presentation is the talent of introducing a message or a product to an audience in the most attractive and convincing way. You can criticize a person and turn it into a conflict without getting your message delivered, and you can criticize the same person in a way that makes him listen to you and understand your point of view smoothly. It is all about how you will do it. If you choose to shout or to use an offensive tone, following an attacking attitude or using some insulting words. Here you go, you choose the first option. This will not end in any desired destination.

If you choose a friendly smiley tone, objective wording and avoided bad feelings. Congratulations, you started a constructive conversation which will absolutely go through smoothly and eventually end up with positive results.

The way you sell it, this is what salespeople do. Did you ever watch a salesman trying to sell a product to someone? They are talented in making this product sounds the best ever. It the art of attracting a person to something in the way that makes his eyes blink, the way that forces his curiosity to know more about it fire up, building up his desire to own it. You could have a brilliant idea, an amazing intention or you are talented in some way. This all doesn't work if you cannot tell anyone about it, you cannot sell what you have.

Think of the most appealing technique when it comes to introducing your work. Not less than 50% of your success is only for your presentation. Think creatively and come up with an extraordinary approach to introduce your ideas to your audience, we don't forget what touches our hearts, what catches our eyes or enlighten our souls. Look around you, you will find a lot of similar products on the market. Most products have an image in our mind. This image is because of how it was presented to consumers. Marketers can easily make a product sound cheap or elite just changing their marketing strategy. Yes, with maybe minor changes in the product itself, professional marketers can manage how people will see and categorize a product following a specially designed marketing strategy for a specific purpose. They manage the impressions they want to leave in customers heads based on strategic business needs. A gift item is not a gift without the wrapping and the ribbon, if you are in a relationship with women or if you are the women, I think you know what that means. Find your own special or alternative way of presenting your idea, product or service to your targeted audience. Your presentation technique is what differentiates you from others, it is what tells your audience about your talent and draws their mental and emotional attention and what gets them attached to what you offer.

Let's take a live example from our modern life, have you ever thought about the difference between Apple iPhone and other products like Samsung competitive smartphones. This is not a technical comparison. However, if you asked technical experts about technical differences without refereeing to what they like or their personal opinions. You will figure out that Samsung along with Google Android has developed a lot of nice, innovative and sophisticated features. Nevertheless, most of the regular users don't know about it. On the other hand, Apple used to introduce a lot of much simpler features, these features are also smart and innovative but are not as sophisticated as in competitor's smartphones. However, most iPhone users are aware of these features and think that nothing is comparable to what they have.

It all goes back to how both companies launch and present their products, Samsung's smartphone launching events used to be deeply technical. These type of presentations are not regular users friendly. Most of the people get out of this presentation under the impression that, ok. They launched a new phone, it looks good and might be interesting. Take any of Apple's iPhone launching events and just watch. The way they speak about what you come up with the new version makes it interesting for anyone to listen. Even if what they are presenting is technically simple in comparison to whatever else in the market, they are talented in making it sounds like the announcing of spaceships for everyone. What touches a women's heart is how you proposed to her, much more than the fact that you actually proposed to her. We see the importance of presentation and marketing in every practice of our lives. Nevertheless, we stay so attached to what we are offering itself more than how are going to offer it. Gather your thoughts in order, build up for new ideas and come up with the extraordinary way approaching your audience. Close your eyes and gather your unforgivable memories in order, awaken this phenomenal feeling inside you and get inspired. Speak like a storyteller, steel people's hearts, and souls and win their full attention. You may have brilliant ideas, but if you can get them to penetrate people's minds, they will not get you anywhere. Don't be shy and don't be hesitant, every idea worth the experience. Don't get into the trap of feeling that something is too odd or not going to work. Steve Jobs said the ones who are crazy enough to think that they can change the world, are the ones who do.

Fruitless Trails (Patience Intelligent)

We don't get to discover new methods, techniques or ideas without experiencing all possibilities. How many times you stopped at the beginning or the middle of your way because of feeling that it is not possible, you can't do it or it is not going to work. Sometimes we don't have enough patience or what I call patience intelligent, we stop before reaching somewhere. Creative thinkers expect fruitless trails, the journey itself is an experience that could lead you to another way. Reaching to a conclusion is better than skipping the experience, a lot of people is guilty of misleading others by saying "I have tried it, and I felt that it is not going to work". If you asked them if they walked through the whole way, they will say no we didn't. Knowing that something is not going to work or something is not going to be fixed in some way is a great knowledge.

Fruitless trails motivate creative people to find alternatives but in this case, they start from a solid base because they know that it didn't work in other ways. You will never get lost or off the track, as long as you are experimental. You walk through the unknowns and accepts failures, fruitless experiences. Being experimental will guide you through the journey to come up with something new, you will be always few steps away from breaking through ordinary outcomes. Patience Intelligent doesn't mean that you should waste your time if you know what you are doing if you love it and if you have the courage to walk the extra mile, you are not wasting your time.

Creative outcomes always worth the efforts, time and the experience. Remember your childhood when you used to learn by experiencing almost everything around, life is the best teacher as long as you attend and experience. Don't give up on your ideas, bring your childish desire to experience all possibilities to the surface, accept and learn

from all outcomes and stay patience
intelligent.

Use the "Nothing to do" breaks to find the way

It is the moment when you are not keen or looking forward doing something, it is the moment when you feel really happy with a crystal clear mind state and vision. Most of the great creative thinks in the mankind history got their one of a kind ideas in the "Nothing to do" breaks. In these moments you see through the darks, you dive deeply into your soul. You will never be closer to the end of the tunnel. Catch the light, collect the dots and make the line. Take the opportunity to meet your feature or to take the decision you never been able to take.

Don't be judgmental

Being judgmental distracts you from understating the difference in others. Creativity is a huge network of ideas and point of views, you don't have the access to all of these when you decide to judge someone's idea or point of view, take the time to explore and understand the difference between where you stand on something and where others stand on the same thing. Sometimes the only issue is that you are looking from the wrong angle.

We are all looking at the same thing but from different perspectives, you don't know whether your side is the perfect spot or not. Creative thinkers, leaders and great innovators pay a lot of attention to what other people think about objects, ideas or products. In the century of information and technology, I can say that as much as information you gain, you get more control of your life, you take better decisions and you learn how to lead and develop great products.

The ability to gain more information about everything is only developed at the moment when you stop being judgmental about different ideas, knowledge, and cultures.

The sky is your limit

Never ask your mind to stop thinking about something because you feel that you cannot change or add more to the subject. It is not that far if you have the courage to walk through, it is not so complicated if you have the desire to fix, it is never too late if you will not waste any more time.

Don't be stopped by your own fears and barriers that you just created in your head, you will never know whether you can or not unless you try it out. If you did it, this will be a great success. If you failed, this will be the best lesson learned.

If you think you have that outstanding thing inside, don't step back and give it a try. If you think you can discover something that no scientist had never find out before, don't waste your time and start right away. If you see yourself as the leader that can develop great business and change people lives, start your way out. When you think that you cannot pass specific limit, don't forget that it was you who defined your own limit. The only proper estimation of where do you stand at any point is to find your way through, the only proper evaluation of your capabilities and powers is when you face your fears, challenges and life obstacles. School marks and written tests don't reflect what you can actually do in real life. Failing in education or not reaching any high ranks is not a prerequisite when it comes to creative thinking, how many scientists from the ones we follow in our life didn't finish or succeed in his education. Learning, reading and seeking more knowledge all the time is perfect. However, you don't have to get a Ph.D. to be creative or to find out something new. Don't listen to yourself or others trying to find out an excuse to stay in the comfort zone doing nothing. The most difficult barriers in your way to success are the ones you create for yourself.

Thinking big should be the trigger for deeper thinking and planning, if you always think big it means that you need to organize yourself and figure out your plan for your dream. It doesn't mean that you should think of smaller or easier ideas. Beware of your steps and make sure you know what to learn, what to do and what not to do. Get the proper helpers, thinkers, and doers. Don't give up your dream, the sky is your limit.

Stay motivated, keep the momentum

Being inspired, having a dream, exploring and passing over the ups and downs, that's a lot. Throughout the way and during your journey, sad moments will come, problems will happen, disappointments and even more. The word stop is most likely to be the only word in a lot of occasions, and you will not see any other option at these times. To keep yourself up and go through the difficult times sometimes it is not enough to be inspired. To continue your way, you need to stay motivated. Learn how to motivate yourself, learn how to see the positive side so you can step forward and not to stop because you are upset or fed up. Motivating yourself starts with doing something that you love to do, buying something that you wanted to buy for yourself, taking a nice break sometimes, up to learning how to control our negative vibes and convert them into positive vibes.

Success journey is not short, motivation is your weapon to survive through the hard times and focuses your attention on your objectives, not on the showstoppers.

If you have a team or other people helping you, that means you need to keep your team motivated as well. Keep your team or the people around you on the same page. Don't forget that the negative vibes are very dangerous. Moreover, being a leader in your journey means that the motivation is always your responsibility. Motivating people is not rocket science if you know these people and you know exactly what you need, and what they need. Listen, understand and react. These are the keys when in it comes to handling other people, get to know what they need, what makes them comfortable and what makes them perform the outstanding performance that you would need. Most of the time people needs are simple and non-tangible. Appreciation, security, and friendship. Get closer to the people around you and categories them according to these emotional groups.

Some people are looking for the appreciation for things they do or feel, this group is sensitive to criticism, blaming or ignoring their emotions. Other people are looking for security, and when we say security we mean to say security in many aspects and forms. Because people are different in the way they live, they are different in their life demands. A leader must add a personal touch to his relationship with his team. This personal touch will give you the access to explore the personal insecurities in others and will help you find out the best way to manage their behavior. Moreover, your personal relationships with the people around you will get exceptionally developed. A true leader will always manage to get this advanced level of people personal relationships and motivation status in which people will be outstandingly performing and encouraged to give unconditionally.

Creativity definition

Creativity is a wide spectrum of arts and beauties. Creativity is a different and special definition of art, it is the art of creating, doing or performing everything, it is the art and beauty which is not necessary to be paints or other forms of artwork. Creativity visualizes the artistic dimension in everything we can do or create. Defining the creativity will open your eyes and makes you see it, it will make you find it in what you do in life, whatever it is. Creativity is to find an alternative, smarter or shorter ways to make things happen in al domains, industries, and human sciences. Don't be stopped by the traditional negative thought that there is no space for creativity in what you do. Sometimes creativity is at your hand while you are looking somewhere else to find it. Remembering this definition enlighten dark areas and will make you see what you do every single day from a different angle. Creativity might be really close to your fingertips.

Ask yourself

Take some off time and remember a car from the 80s and compare it with a new car, remember how the first phone looked like and compare it with our new phones or probably smartphones. Finally, find a picture of a school class in the 80s and compare it with school classes nowadays, have you ever thought about this. Everything has changed but not the way we educate our kids, isn't that alerting? It is a shame that we always think the same way when it comes to helping our kids find their ways in their lives. Why are we tighten them to grades and marks and putting them in the situation where they have to be evaluated based on the things they cannot do. Isn't it like judging the lion for its disability to fly?

Ask yourself all these questions and remember, we decide to kill the creativity inside our souls every day. Not only that, we are happily killing it on the inside of the new generations as well thinking that we are doing the right thing.

Always remember that negativity is like an infection, it is like a disease which can spread in many ways and has variant symptoms and deeply impacts people minds and souls. Whenever you get infected by the negative vibes, read this book again and don't get distracted by life issues. You don't need a doctor to face such disease, it is a disease which you can easily decide to heal your soul of.

Empower yourself, enlighten your soul and awaken your creativity engine deep inside you, right before it dies.

The time game

Whenever you think that nothing is going to be changed, be confident that it's wrong. read in history or search the internet and find out a huge number of documentaries and other materials about how we used to do things in the past and how are doing the same things today. Take a deep breath and think deeply of the things that your grandfathers or the people before us used to say that these things are impossible, while we can do these things now with a touch of a button. Look at the world social and political situations and remember that some years back a lot of the scenarios we are living today we had never dreamed they someone will even think of them. Time is the only constant in life, everything is possible to be changed with time but not the time itself. Time has two main roles the play of life, time is playing the good and the bad friend. Time is the alliance and the enemy.

Nature, animals, people life and people themselves, sciences and technologies and everything else in our lives has changed and will keep on changing more and more over time. In 2017, I can say that the most powerful weapon on earth is time. Everybody is around us is playing the time game. In everyday life we hear "to buy more time", "they cannot wait for more time", and "it will be changed by the time". The time game is not an easy one, you need to be prepared. Always remember that time is your alliance if you utilized it in your favor. Time is your enemy if you let it pass without a plan or a reaction to control the outcomes of all other variable parameters around time. If you lose in the time game you lose in the life game, you lose your control over everything that can be changed over time. This means you lose everything. Negative thoughts like nothing can be changed or I cannot do it, are just the beginning of the wrong track. Self-confidence, positive and creative thinking are the circumstances that you should keep maintained during time game. This will push you to the finish line on "time". The time at which your desired outcomes are logically achieved. Your life or career goals are on the timeline if you managed that timeline in the proper way. Time is a train with an endless line of stations if you don't manage the time "the timeline" you will not reach any of your desired stations. According to the game rules, you will stay in the beginning, where you are or in nowhere.

Money game

If you don't have money you will not be able to reach anywhere! Have you heard this before? You will defiantly hear this all the time and almost from everyone around you. It is not that the money isn't important or not necessary, it is about how you should handle a financial limitations issue or situation. Money is the water for business and life, nothing is alive without water. Money can highly impact life or projects in both the negative and the positive ways. Nevertheless, it is not a barrier. Most of the people listed on the world list of wealthy people didn't have any money when they started. They knew how to start with minimal resources, they knew how to invest and increase the value of things they do or provide for their customers. Always remember the baby steps, babies cannot walk directly when they want to do it, they crawl first. This means that they are flexible to compromise the things they want but they are not able to do and do other things they can do as a start. Steps are very important if you don't want to fall off the ladder, steps are good to review the journey and perfect decision gates for what you do.

If you have a big idea or project that would require some financial resources that you don't have now, you either think of an alternative "Creative" way of doing the same thing at lower cost, or you think of something else to you can do that will help you increase your financial capabilities. Never compromise your big dream because of money, money isn't an easy game, but it is always possible to find your way out.

Read and learn more about financial and money management, this will help develop your money handling skills. Money management skills will help add a huge value to your personal and professional lives. There are a lot of scientific techniques that will help you enhance your money spending habits, savings and investments strategies and most importantly cash flow management. Can you imagine your life without water, if you have limited water resources then you need to consider your water usage seriously so you maintain the amount of available water to be used? Money is that important for your business or your personal life, that's why you need to learn how you manage cash resources carefully, efficiently and practically. Without a proper cash planning and management, you will not be able to sustain your business or day to day life.

Money is not only the cash, or liquid financial assets, money is also other on hand resources. Resources could be materials, human resources!! Yes, human resources are also great assets if they can help to generate other resources or products. All resources which can be used to produce a product or to perform a service are money. If all of these resources are managed properly you can always sustain and maintain your steps forward to your objectives. All resources are beneficial if you know how to use them if you don't look at them as cost or loss. Each situation has its own circumstances where resources benefits or values may defer according to other factors.

Look at what you have from different angles and evaluate carefully, you might be losing a lot of opportunities because of a negative situation or negative mindset. Opportunities are always there if we only know how we can use the resources around us, resources of all types because all resources are money and money is like water for life.

Skills game

The non-physical resources, it all what you can do or perform so you get rewarded in return. Everyone has his own skill sets, everyone has something to stand out. Doctors have their own required skill set, like researching, analyzing symptoms and people feelings to diagnose a disease, engineers have also their own required skills like problem-solving, analytical thinking and planning. All skills can be further developed even if you are good at what you do, there is always room for more. Don't stay where you are, don't think you have enough experience or knowledge, always seek for development. Whatever your skill is, you always can do it better or add something new to it. Everyday life is full of opportunities that we don't utilize, new things that we can learn about or new things we can do.

The skills game is linked to the money game, directly and indirectly, developing your skills will open the door for higher financial returns, developing your skills will enlighten your mind for new perspectives. In both ways, you will tend to perform better, give more or do the extraordinary thing.

Everything in life is for a price, developing your skills is like earning extra money so you can buy much more expensive things you had never been able to buy. Reaching to the excellence level will grant you the green card to the world of qualities. This green card has its requirements and pre-requisites, requirements are the intention to play a skills game and your strong desire to win.

You have only one way to achieve a lifelong pass to this world, keep on playing the game.

The edge game (I am different)

After you explore, identify and develop your skills, you need to take this to another level. Find out your edge, it is the edge level.

All doctors can do diagnosis, surgeries and health consultations. All engineers can do drawings, designs and engineering consultations. All bakers can back, all chefs can cook. Boring right!

Do you see how many people doing the same thing that you do; can you imagine that you are not doing anything differently. Here is where the edge game must start, finding the alternative way or finding that different thing that you can add to whatever you do so you make your own blueprint.

If you read the previous barograph starting with "All doctors" with an eye open to positive thinking, some good things will cross your mind. You will probably remember a doctor who is different from the others, it could be also that chef who makes the unforgivable taste. There are people in this world who won the edge game and reached where they can add something new to what they do, or maybe doing the same thing in an alternative way.

Don't stop before you figure out your special thing, that special thing is your key to win the edge game and achieve outstanding results in your life. Doing things the same way as others do might be good enough for a constant income and ordinary life. It is only that simple tough that could change the picture from an outdoor capture to an eye-catching scenery.

Your edge could be your experience, your own special skill or your own unique technique to handle what you do. Everyone has that special touch, everyone can add a great contribution to what we do every day, the chance is always there. The decision starts within your soul, it is your desire to find your edge. How many chefs or baker decided to create a new recipe or revamp an existing meal and what he did succeed and made him worldwide fame. What has changed is how people feel or think about their food or how they eat. A lot of people can cook, and a lot of others do that every day, but not everyone decided to find out where they can achieve the exceptional results. Not everyone has the courage to change what others do or adding his touch and get to explore the extraordinary.

The edge game is crucial for your creative journey, you cannot think creatively without playing this game, you cannot change your life without fining the keys to win it. A decision not to stick to what everybody around is doing is all that it takes to start. This decision could be one of the most important and life-changing decisions you have ever taken in your life, you don't need anyone else except yourself to think and step forward in taking this decision. No knows what you do better than yourself, no one knows where you can exceed everyone's expectations except you. Deep inside you have the answer, deep inside you have the treasure locked, deep inside is where the game begins. Play the edge game and find out that thing that can be added to the recipe to change this ordinary taste completely and take the bite to a different level. Find out the missing to solve a problem, find out the missing to make the picture an eye-opener. Don't stop playing this game, it is endless.

Accept unplanned outcomes and accidents

Don't stop explore and doubt, contradict
yourself every now and then

Don't be shy to be the child inside your soul

Start the creative thinking engine inside you
before it dies

References

Branson, Richard, 2012. Richard Barson Bares His Business Secrets.

Csikszentmihalyi, Mihaly, 1996. Creativity. USA: HarperCollins.

Feynman, Richard, 1994. No Ordinary Genius: The Illustrated Richard Feynman.

Morais, Fernando, 2010. Paulo Coelho: A Warrior's Life

Samuelson, Paul A., 1970. How I Became an Economist.

Tharp, Twyla, 2002. The Creative Habit: Learn IT and Use it for Life.

Judkins, Rod. The Art of Creative Thinking, 2015.

Ahmed M. Sonbol
2018